The Watercycle Ride

By

Richard Tysoe

Date of Publication
April 1997

First Published 1992
ISBN: 0 9522876 0 9

Published by:
Richard Tysoe
5, Warden Abbey
1 Bedford MK41 0SW

Poems and pictures copyright
© Richard Tysoe 1992

Printed by:
ProPrint
Riverside Cottage
Great North Road
Stibbington
Peterborough PE8 6LR

ISBN: 0 9522876 2 5

INTRODUCTION

This is a book for children of all ages (say from 5 to 100, give or take a few). It begins as spring is stirring, and follows through the year: through March winds, April rains, the summer holidays: through autumn leaves drifting, and into deep winter, ending at the start of spring again.

It is not all weather, though it has a lot of that. Some days are for playing around, some are for going to school. Animals and birds are part of all our lives: so are light and darkness, imagination, fear, wonder and having fun; but without that amazing watercycle, none of us would be here for any rides!

Beginning in the End

The wind beats at the barren hedges,
Straggly grey-green grasses sifting:
Seeking the last year's blackened leaves there,
Tied down to tangles, no more drifting.
Sort wind, sift wind, blow so cold!
For there's nothing left of the year grown old.

The piercing steel of the February wind
Probes through our woollen armour now:
Slices at hands in the intact gloves.
And it moans at the trees, but the trees won't bow.
It sulks over shrinking pits of snow;
And there's little left for the wind to blow.

Is winter king of the hillside rows?
They will shake their twigs, but they won't bow down!
And the hedges know that the sun is for them:
Down in the stocks, under twigs so brown
There are stretching buds that are showing green!
Deep in the hedge there is life unseen!

Birds that flocked to the woodland margin,
Stripping the twigs of the winter's store
Scatter themselves in the sun-bright mornings
Busy with bustle and song once more.
Biting, the wind while the numb Earth slumbered,
See, but the biting days are numbered!

THE GUSTY WIND

Shake the windows!
Slam the gates!
Break the branches on the way!
I'll huff and I'll puff
And I'll blow your house in!
I'll shout down the chimney
And make such a din!
Break the windows!
Snatch the slates!
I'm a troublesome wind today!

Trees in the Wind

Black, twiggy fingers grope the sky,
Roaring that the wind should cease
Bending and twisting,
Buffeting and breaking
Their knobby, black elbows,
And leave them in peace!

Wind in the Town

Rattling windows, and sweeping the streets
Scattering litter wherever it goes,
Flattening fences, and snatching at skirts,
Blustery bother it blows!
All of the paper is bumbled along,
Scattered about, whisked all about,
People's umbrellas are turned inside out,
Buffeted by the wind!

The Storm Wind

I am the wind, riding high,
Swirling through the sky,
Driving the clouds like herds of cattle before me,
Hurling the rain before me!
Bow down, you trees!
Twigs to the ground, or I'll snap you, crack!
Nothing can stand my attack!

Wind and Rain

Wind, wind, running through the sky
Playing with the shirts and skirts
To make the washing dry,
Funny how you bring the clouds
To make it wet with rain,
Funny how you take the wet
And make it dry again.

Wind, wind, blowing on the sea,
Picking up the cloudy mist
To tipple rain on me -
Wind, wind, give it all a rest!"
Warm and sunny summer days
Are what I like the best!

BATTLING THE AIR

The roaring wind buffets my body
And blows me, wobbling on two wheels
Now at the verge, now into road!
My moped stutters, its engine strains,
Gargling small against the gale
That rushingly swallows it sound!
I sit tense, touching the brakes,
Balancing, feet akimbo to catch
The gusts and the buffets that beat at my going
And the wind, the bully, hits me hardest
Where hedges are not, and fields are bare.
There he holds and halts me in the road,
And blasts me with pellets of rain in the face.
Shall I get home? I will get home!
With home my target I gargle on.

KITE

With angry, rattling growls it faces the gusting wind,
Rearing with swelling pride, higher and higher,
Its several traily tails lash and turn and twist,
As it pitches, dips and wrestles with the gusty air,
It pulls at the tight and tugging cord
Which goads it into action, climbing:
It snarls, demanding more and more!
Pull! release- now up, and up! -
Mad dip and dive! Tails twirl and up again!
'Let me up! Let me at it!' the kite demands,
Growling proudly, lashing tails,
'Let me rise above this air!
More rope! more room! give me more!'
I pull, I pay out the restraining wire
Tying the kite to me and earth,
But without which it would never fly.

The Waking of the World

Wake up World! Wake up trees!
Stretch your buds to green!
Wake up, trees! Open your fair
Bright blossoms to be seen!
Dark and tight your buds have been
All the winter long.
Can't you see the sun is out?
Can't you hear the song?
Open your blossoms, pink and white,
Smile in the sunshine, glow in the light!
Morning is here, it's Spring, you know -
Stretch your buds and grow!

The Primula

From the crispy, crinkled lettuce leaves
A bright face looks out.
Five bright petals surround
A sunny yellow eye.
Like arms flung wide to welcome,
Like a radiant smile.
The primula perks up frost-bound February
And promises Spring quite soon.
Bunched beside its bold, bright innocence,
Shyer brothers and sisters huddle
Waiting their turn
Each to fling wide their welcoming smile.

Sparrows at Dawn

Like sad grey tennis balls, lodged in the spaces
Under the gutterings and all high places,
Feathers fluffed against the frost, the wind in our faces,
Songless and sad we sit, waiting for the morning,
Hoping for breakfast on a cold day dawning.

Mistle Thrush

Little Miss Mistle Thrush
Quick hop! still -
Listen: dip! catch a worm,
Snatch it with the bill!
Long legs, streaky skirt
Skip - hop - freeze!
Eyes bright, all alert.
Fly off to the trees!

Before the Dawn

In soft darkness a songbird sings,
Sweetly, liltingly, lovingly, a song of light:
Night music, melody without shadow,
Lifting me listening to share in the joy of his singing,
While the whole world sleeps.
Alone he sings; a song of hope,
A lifting of the heart in the stillness around.
Clear notes of daylight brighten the warm, dark night
Till a pale edge lifts the curtain of the sky
And smaller, sleepy cheeping joins his tune:
A rustling, twittering small-voiced chorus
Hurry along like a woodland stream;
A happy chattering, twinkling throng
Tune up their throats and join in song
To greet the dawn: and morning comes.
Come on, day. The birds are ready for you.

Daffodils

Bright sunlight, on a morning
                crisp and cool
Sparkles on the grass of the
              small front gardens.
The fresh spring air
              cuts down the street
Past the raised, bright faces,
           the sunny heads
Of the daffodils: who nod to the breeze
As if to say, 'Good morning. Happy Easter!'

Bedford Park Lake

Gulls wheel above the pond,
A lake alive with busy birds,
Skimming, swimming, dappling its brimming
Edge, and rippling the crowded surface.
The ripples run wider,
Rings brown against the blue
Reflection of the sky;
Ripples crossing, twinkling blue light.
A busy lake, where all is movement:
Ducks, at speed across the surface
Glide (patrol?) in arrow form:
No doubt the lake belongs to them.
The stately swans ignore them.
These dip their necks in quiet contemplation.
A moorhen wobbles at the water's edge,
Teetering on the bank
(As if forced to walk the plank!)
A gull swoops in- applies his brakes-
Hangs low in the air and
Ploughs the lake with forward feet:
And from a plane becomes a ship,
Floating, and at peace.

WELLIES

In the mud my wellies stand—
Mud is trouble when you're small—
Gripped as in a sticky hand.
In the mud I stand and bawl.
On this treacly, tricky track
Mud is plastered to my knees.
I shall want my wellies back!
Someone come and help me, please!

The Bulldozers

The land here has belonged to roots
And buds and flowers, and fresh green shoots
Since time began, and worms have chewed
The silent soil, and found their food
In deepest darkness. Now the lid
Is lifted off from what they did,
As bulldozers snarl, as they
Gnaw at the ground,
And they rip out the roots
With a roaring of sound!
The sweetly green meadow
Is churned into black
And flowers mixed to mud
In a spin-wheeled attack!
While diesel fumes poison
The air all the day,
There are creatures made homeless.
The birds fly away.

SLIDE INTO NIGHT

Midnight.
All was silent save the ticking clock
Whose scratchy, rhythmic movement
Soothed the night.
Darkness.
Deep darkness filled the room.
And beside the great wardrobe
A blackness hung -
Like a hole with no edges,
Deeper than a dark cave.
What was in that shadow hole?
And where was the wall,
And the lightswitch?
And as I looked
And looked, and saw nothing,
A rustling sound
Moved out on me!
A noise like the wardrobe being
Dragged aside
Grew to the roaring of an express train
Or an avalanche!
And the bed slid lightly
From underneath the eiderdown
Which bumped gently to the floor.

(In the night, senses are sharper, so sounds seem louder. The noise that frightened me was the sound of the quilt sliding off the bed.)

Tremors

A thunderous knocking
Broke my slumber!
Slowly I raised my head.
A rattling slam
Then shook the house,
And a bumping, clonking
    Window-shaking
        Shattering
        Battering
            Set me a-quivering,
            Burrowing down into bed!
And the thudding,
Bumping,
    Troublesome tramping
        Stamping came near!
I trembled in fear
As the doors all shook,
And the windows rattled!
    Pictures tumbled
    Off the wall!
    And the shaking
        Thudding
            Stopped in the hall.
              Then, with a bash!
              And a splintering crash!
              The door flung wide,
                  And there stood outside
                  The towering,
                      Darkening

                      Looming,

                        Tremendous

                          BULK –

Of Uncle Fred.

So I got up and made a cup of tea.

My Balloon

Zip it went
Out of my hand,
　　　Whizzing around
The startled room.
　Heads turned.

My balloon
　　　Buzzed all about
All around.
　　　Up at the top
　　　　Burnt itself out

　　　And flopped.

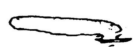

The Concrete Mixer

His mouth is open, round and wide -
With a sloshing and a grinding sound
He chews the rattling pebbles inside
And chomps them round and around.
How he shakes and shudders with a rattling roar!
As they feed him sand on a spade!
Now his mouth is full, and he can't take more,
But he'll chew it till the concrete's made.

Journey of a Puddle

If I were a puddle in the street,
I shouldn't wait for the wind or heat
Of the sun to warm or fry me dry
Till my puddling days were done, not I!

I'd creep or swim to the nearest drain-
Before the sun, straight after the rain-
Then strike out boldly for river or sea.

The only places where puddles are free!
I'd leave the gutters and streets behind me,
And hide in the deep where the sun couldn't find me!

Fishing

I made a kite, to fly it high
And carry up a net,
To fish up in a mackerel sky.
I wondered, was it wet?
I thought a cloud upon my wall
Would be a lovely thing!
I couldn't reach the sky at all-
I hadn't got the string!

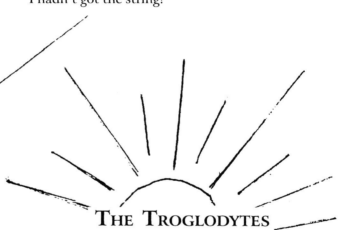

The Troglodytes

Bright is the sun,
Dazzling bright!
It hurts our eyes with its
Brilliant light!
We'll pull down the blinds
And sit in the gloom.
We can't have such light
Disturbing the room!

Wet Days

On cold days and wet,
When the sun seems to hide,
It's nice to forget
All the cold outside.
And you don't have to look
At the rain out there,
You can sit with a book
And your feet in a chair.
Let the drops bounce high,
Let them gurgle down the spout!
While we sit in the dry
Till the sun comes out.

The Puddle Pounce

I'm just a puddle
Staring at the sky
Thinking nothing
Lying in the road till a car drives by
Then I -
Leap in a sheet
On the passers-by
At the side of the street
To share with them
My cold and icy
Wetness! And a load
Of dirty bits I picked up in the road!

STEPPING STONES

In the yard there's a puddle
Very wide, very wet.
And we've spread bricks and boulders-
All across it they are set.
Now, step to the first stone
Then onto the brick.
Careful not to fall!
Spread your arms, that's the trick.
Don't put your feet in water-
Falling in makes you out!
And your Mum will give you trouble
With her tongue or with a clout!
Now, step- hold your wobble!
Keep your balance as you go:
It's a rather slippy cobble
And it's very wet below!
So step very steady!
There are only two more blocks.
Last leap! And you've done it now,
With dry shoes and socks!

THUNDERCLOUD

There's an evil wizard in a cloud-shaped aeroplane
Coloured like the night as he rumbles overhead.
All the people under think it's just the noise of thunder.
With a bright
        FLASH OF LIGHT
                      he could strike them
                                    all dead!
But the people don't die as he hurries with the breeze,
And nobody sees as the cloud rumbles by.

ACCIDENT IN THE SKY

The stickiness and heat,
Trickling sweat across his brow,
Collecting at his eyebrows,
Caused the angel to stumble -
Tearing down the curtain of heaven
In searing light!
He fell against a mountain of piled pots and pans
Whose clash and sudden clamour
Clanged, boomed and rolled,
Trundling away to the corners of the sky:
While spots of rain
Spilled from the punctured clouds.

Wet Homecoming

The light turns yellow, while the air goes still.
And the air seems sticky, and the day grows dark.
All the leaves on the trees in the street seem to whisper,
With not the slightest breath of wind to rustle in the boughs.
Then the raindrops spit a dotty pattern on the ground
And we hurry for the shelter of our own front door.
There's a rumbling murmuring somewhere in the sky.
There's a fumbling of keys, as we huddle at the door.
And we're glad to be home, and we're glad to be dry
As the rain pours down, as the street turns black,
And the puddles glare back at the darkening sky
With a flicker on their faces as the drops all bounce.
'Oh, it's nice to be back, just listen to the rain!'
'Oh, it's good to be home! Let's have a cup of tea.
Let it rain, let it rain! Will you put the kettle on?'

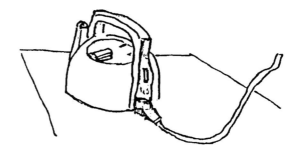

GARDEN BIRDS

Sparrows shout their sharp demands:
'Chips!' they order, 'chips!' but come for bread.
The robin's liquid, lilting, thrilling song
Sweetly rippling from a roof or fence
Belies to us his swift aggressiveness.
He sings, 'Keep off, this patch is mine!'
To birds who understand the music's words.
The gentle blackbird hammers its alarm
Like short nails into brick, so sharp repeating.
Calm down, my friend: my dog presents no danger!
Sing us your sweeter evening song,
That soulful, melancholy, longing chant
Whose blue notes slip such magic in the scale.
Other birds, mysterious in the trees
Pump tyres, no doubt for quicker getaway,
As starling hooligans home on the grass
To steal from fellows food that each has found;
For stolen food is better, sweeter meat
Than that which lies in plenty on the ground.

Suburban Caterpillar

*(The lackey moth caterpillars that kept escaping
from the vivarium reminded us of an electric train
by their appearance and the way they moved.)*

It rattles by without a sound.
To pick up power, we may be sure,
From hidden lines within the ground
Its orange whiskers sweep the floor.
At speed across the room it moves,
Commuter of the Hawthorn Line.
Heedless of human feet it proves
And fearless of this hand of mine.
I lay a twig across its track
To trip my caterpillar train.
It soon derails. I take it back
And put it in the tank again.

THE WATERCYCLE

Winds whisk the water up,
Take it from the sea,
Turn it into vapour
Where the clouds blow free.
Can you ride a water cycle?
Ride it in the sky?
Is the saddle wet as the clouds ride high?

Hills turn the wind,
Drive it higher in the air.
Clouds have to rise,
And it's cold up there.
Can you ride a water cycle,
Rain upon the hills?
Do the brakes work when the wet sky spills?

Land soaks the puddles up
Deep into the ground,
Where the dark lakes drip
That the people haven't found.
Can you ride a water cycle
Out into the light?
Where the bright stream trickles, are the wheels all right?

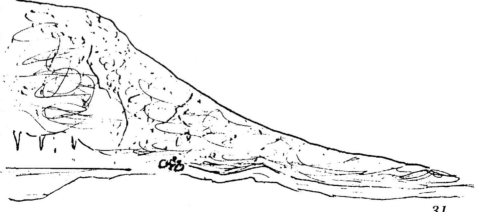

Streams fill the rivers and the lakes of the land:
And the pumps, and the taps,
And the washbasin stand.
Can you ride a water cycle,
Trickle down the drain?
Would the spokes need cleaning in the river once again?

Rivers wander, rippling
Till they meet the tide
Where the salt waves wash
At the ocean side.
Can you ride a water cycle
As you leave the land?
Do the tyres need pumping in the pebbles and the sand?

Winds whisk the water up,
Take it from the sea:
Turn it into vapour
Where the clouds blow free.
The sun can ride a water cycle
All around the planet.
No-hands he has pedalled since the Father first began it.

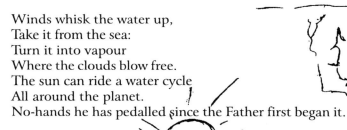

The Dream of the Sea

We drift
On the chest of the sea,
A vast, slumbering animal,
Rising and falling
In steady rhythm.
He sleeps,
A shimmering giant,
Stretched out flat and far,
Twinkling,
Like countless stars
As far as the distant line
Where the sky comes down.
No sound. Or is there
Whispering, towards the land
Among the sand and rocks?
And what would he talk about, the sea?
Of men in their matchwood boats? not he!
Then, what does he talk about,
And who is it hears?
His speech is slow, and low, and deep
For human ears.
        In the rumbling dashing
        Of waves washing across the rocks
        He speaks to the land,
        To the sand,
        To the cliffs.
        He whispers that he knew their fathers,
        Mighty mountains
        Higher than they
        Harder than they,
        Greater, and greyer, and grimmer than they
        In the days when nothing
        Walked.

Those aged mountains never shook
With his furious, lashing
Waves dashing against them.
They stood
And took it.
And in gentler mood
He would slap and tickle them,
Filch the pebbles from their caves,
Undermine
Their stern, unbending confidence
Till they fell
And cracked,
And crumbled,
And were washed to sand.

And the rocks and cliffs of the land
Stand
And take his mocking:
And pretend not to see
The bits that he knocks off,
The sand that he filches from their feet.

He sleeps.
But his fingers never rest,
Caressing the shores
As he whispers
And dreams
Of the times he has seen.

The Global View

The world is round. I flick my fins
And cruise from end to end,
And gaze beyond the glass, where giant
Human forms are moving past
In airy emptiness, outside the world.
The world is round. I have explored
Its trailing weeds, know every stone:
And understand the natural things,
Like food floating on the skyward side.
The world is round. I am alone,
The round world's sole inhabitant:
Though ghostly giants' gaping faces
Press in close, then fade away,
Lost in the misty nothingness.
Alone. The purpose of my world.
I flick my fins, and cruise again.

Swan on the Falls

From the bridge in foot-hot summer
We envy him, the silent swan
As he stands at the sweeping-by
Top of the falls.
Clear water washes his summer-cool feet
To fall in foam from step to step,
Thunderous, frothy, white and tumbling,
Roaring away in a shout of sound
That stills our minds. We stand there watching
The patient, peaceful long-necked wader
All intent on the speeding stream;
And from the bridge, we share his peace
As in our minds we stand with him.

The Minnow

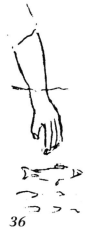

I didn't see him at first,
Brown and motionless against the stones,
Carved out of stone himself, it seemed,
But alive, and moving in the water,
Fins flickering ever so slightly
As the running stream rippled over.
Alive, was he, or dead?
I dipped my hand into the icy stream
And he vanished.
One swift kick of his tail
And he appeared a yard away
From the memory my fingers almost touched.

THE SWALLOW

(This bird was resting at night, very still, in the porch above the front door)

Tireless flight
Chasing prey
All the day
Until the night
The swallow flits,
Whirls and dodges;
Till he lodges
Where he sits
All alone
In our portal,
Living mortal
Still as stone.
It gives us cheer
That one so free
And swift as he
Should stay so near:
We feel aglow.
He has our love.
He sits above
And doesn't know.

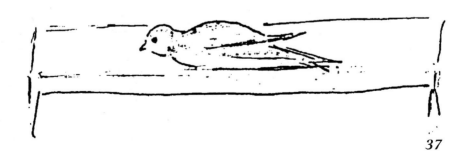

Terry the Terrible

When Terry the Terrible goes to the shops
All that should happen there suddenly stops.
Maybe a shelf of cakes suddenly drops,
Scattering cardboard and cooking!
All of the customers cringe at the sound -
Stare at the packages spread on the ground -
Hope it's not their kid who's fooling around!
(All he was doing was looking!)

Surly Riser

If you wish to catch the milkman,
You must rise quite early.
You may not find his temper sweet,
For at that time he's surly.
Can you wonder that he hardly
Reads the notes you leave him?
Folks who chop and change their order
Only vex and grieve him.

Gooseberry Jam

Jam gets into awkward places,
Sticks to fingers, sticks to faces,
Gooseberry jam is very sticky.
Too far up the spoon it reaches!
Wonder what it is that teaches
Gooseberry jam to be so tricky?

High Summer

On this hot summer day I'm lazing on the lawn
Hiding from the burning sun in the sky,
Who searches for garden plants to shrivel
With scorching heat. The plum tree flutters
Protecting shadow on wilting pansies
Caught in the patches of pulsing, brilliant light.
In my brows sweat trickles, as tickling wasps,
Flies and bees buzz about my head.
They dive in my drink and try to drown:
I lose it on the lawn to save their lives.
I hide beneath my hat, and fold away
The dazzling page of depressing news,
And close my hurting eyes to the heat of day.

Riverside Blues

I went for a swim in the river,
Which chilled me right through to my liver.
I found my clothes gone,
I could put nothing on,
So I just had to stand there and shiver!

The Rubble-Bubble Bounce

My garden was covered in rubble
Which gave me a whole lot of trouble.
I wrapped it in rope,
And I scrubbed it with soap
And blew it away in a bubble.

This rubble that caused me such pain
Is giving me trouble again!
Now see where it went
Now its motion is spent,
And it's sitting there blocking the drain!

SOLOMON STRONG

Solomon Strong
Was a singer of song
Whose strength was a special feature.
Once he stripped the string
From his strumming thing
To strangle a stroppy, striped creature.

(This was probably a Tasmanian pit-bull wombat).

SAUSAGES

Sunshine so hot!
Eye-blinding bright and hot.
The sky-level grill
Bakes down on
Barbecuing bodies on the beach.
Turn, you silly sausages, turn
And cook the other side!
Move about like the kids,
And cool yourselves in the sea!
But the sausages slumber,
Baking a brighter sunburn
All one side.

MR. HEDGEHOG ON THE BEACH

People say holidays should be fun.
Why am I sitting down here in the sun
All alone with the sand and the sea?
Why isn't James sitting here with me?
Noisy, big people are playing at ball.
No-one will notice a hedgehog at all!
Why do I sit by a hole in the sand?
Where are the family? I don't understand.
While James was digging, I sat here with him.
Someone said something like 'Come for a swim.'
Now I'm alone. They just left me here lying.
Jamie, come back! Your poor hedgehog is crying!

House Mouse

People's houses are made for mice:
Cavity walls are a piece of cake!
We can go through the smallest holes
Into your cupboards, the food to take.
    Running up inside your wall -
    You might hear our scrabbling feet.
    You can lock your food away, but
    If there's anything to eat,
    You be sure we mice'll find it:
    Cake crumbs, pet food, we don't mind it!

Behind the cooker's a cosy place;
Back of the 'fridge' is rather good.
Kitchen cupboards are rather sweet;
We love to be warm, and near your food.
    In your kitchen late at night
    We can sniff and find our meat.
    Paper packets are no problem
    Round the food we like to eat.
    Jars and tins frustrate us, sure:
    We prefer a crumb-strewn floor.

The Cat

In the dark, the cat waits.
Eyes that watch the tiny gap
In the skirting board, in the darkened room:
Ears alert for a scratch or tap.
Wait, Watch, Watch the hole!
Only a cat can wait that way!
Soft to step in the midnight kitchen,
Crouching, creeping, claws away:
Eyes on the hole in the darkest corner,
Ears all alert for that tiny sound.
Tense as a trap that springs execution!
Smallest of squeals!
And the supper's found.

The Woolywoofer

My dog is a woolly pom-pom
With shaggy eyebrows
Hiding merry brown eyes.
There's a long nose
Tipped with shiny black,
And a happy smile
Over chin whiskers soaked in gravy:
A sweeping-brush tail:
And feet that jump all over you
And anyone who comes.

Rabbits

Thanks for the rabbits that scamper in the fields
(Though the farmer thinks they're a pest!).
Just sitting and list'ning at evening light,
Whiskers atwitch, and ears upright,
Or chasing in circles, their tails bobbing white,
Rabbits, I think, are best!

Dusk

On the wings of the wind
At the heels of the day
Night comes.
'Hurry home!' whispers the wind.
Night comes quickly,
Riding on the clouds,
Chasing the longest
Fleeing shadows of the sun.
Slate-blue fingers stretch across the sky.
'Quick, quick, quick!' an anxious blackbird calls
As little creatures scurry to their nests.
Night is coming
Swiftly on the wind.
Hurry! hurry home!

TREEBOP

Rain rattled against my window
As thrown by an invisible hand.
I looked out on a dreary day
And I saw that the trees were dancing!
There in my garden, I saw them sway.
The garden was having a party!
The uncut grass danced a disciplined formation;
The young fruit trees formed a graceful set,
Bowing and swaying with stately grace;
The shrubs and flowers in the borders
Seethed party excitement,
While the big, old apple tree at the distant end
Hand-jived by himself, heedless of all other.
They danced to the music of the wind.
I could not hear the band,
But their vocalist sang down my chimney.
Moany and sad the song I heard-
Though merrily outside they jived,
While that vandal hurled handfuls at my window!

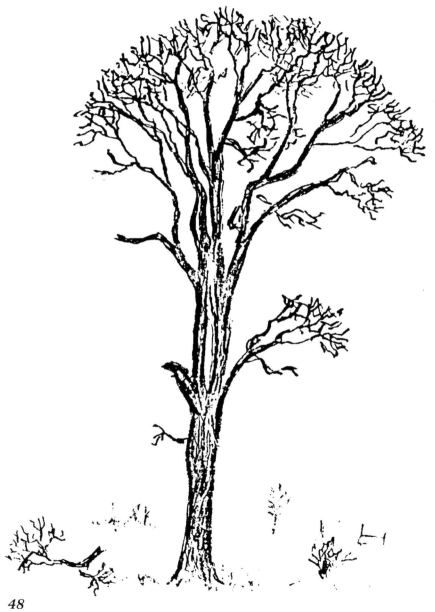

The Elm Tree's Doom

Straight arms, strong arms, twiggy, lifeless,
Long arms reaching to the sky.
Down near the ground green buds appear,
But no sap flows in the trunk this year
And the white cross dooms it to die.

Marked with a cross! and a popping choking
Rises to a roaring bray!
And the whirling, biting, tearing wheel
Roars like a pain that the tree should feel
In its fibres savaged away!

Stoic stands the dying elm tree,
Gothic branches never sway.
'Let this screaming demon tear-
His roaring sawing I can bear!
I will stand here! He'll go away!'

Slow the sway with no returning;
Branches rake the uncaring sky.
Splintering, groaning, topple slow,
Then faster to the ground below!
Crashing branches! There to lie.
Timber! There to lie.

STARLIGHT

Light from a star,
Long ago light
A hundred years coming
To reach my sight.
And now that I see it,
Does it still shine
For stargazers after
This life of mine?
God only knows now
The ends of the sky.
The star's in his hands now
And so am I.
Both ends are held in
His knowledge and sight,
A faster connection
Than time or light.

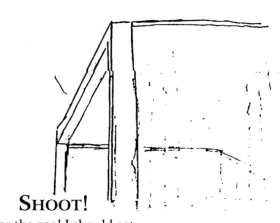

SHOOT!

As I aimed for the goal I should get
I slipped on the grass (which was wet),
The ball trickled wide,
I went into a slide,
And my boots hit the back of the net!

Autumn Leaves

From side to side
It slips through the air
Like a boat at the fair
Giving someone a ride:
A crinkly craft,
As it falls to the ground
With a tinkling sound,
And is rolled by the draught
To the side of the street,
To join all the others,
Its crumbling brothers,
All crunched by the feet
Of the children who pass.
All fair summer's weather
They'd whispered together
As green as the grass
As they hung on the bough
Of their motherly tree -
Who at length cut them free,
Not needing them now.

Autumn Scrunch

We shuffle and crunch
Through a beautiful carpet
Of scattered and crumbling
Skittling leaves.
Bright ones, yellow ones,
Russet and rustling
Red ones, stripy ones:
So glorious a carpet
Only the Earth
Could afford it.
We scrunchily scuffle
And pick up the pretty ones,
Bright ones, patterned ones,
Carry them home.
Fine in the lines of their coloured beauty,
Treasures of the woods, we carry them home
When the carpeted grass
Out-twinkles the sober, grey sky.

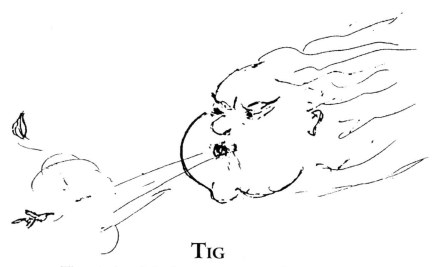

Tig

The wind and the leaves are out to play.
Run, leaves, run, or he'll blow you away!
Scampering, giggling, round and round,
Hiding in heaps where they'll never be found,
Dashing in doorways, and under the stairs,
Safe into corners where nobody cares!
Those that he touches, he tosses aside.
Some of them whirl away, gone for a ride!
Run, leaves, run, or he'll whisk you away!
Scatter, and gather wherever you may!

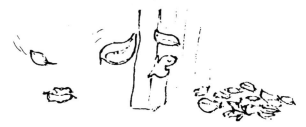

THE CLASSROOM GHOST

I'm the wicked classroom ghost
The one the teachers fear the most.
Around the taps I leave a puddle.
I leave the books all in a muddle!
And when I shout or make a noise,
The teacher always blames the boys!
I steal the papers from each drawer
And scatter them about the floor.
I move the bags to where I choose
And trip up teachers with your shoes!
I switch the coats and bags on pegs,
I clatter chairs on table legs,
And no-one, no-one knows it's me-
They only blame the folks they see!

LONDON FIRE

Leaping, flickering, crackling flames
Roar in rage to the smoke-filled sky,
Spitting out sparks with the hate of battle.
Run, little people from the red, mad ogre!
Eating all the houses, burning all the city,
Roofs all blazing, black timbers rattling!
Scream, little people! See if it can stop him!
What use are buckets when the water pipe's dry?
Smoke is going to choke you, ashes going to roast you,
Flames going to snatch you, leap across and catch you!
Run, little people, run where you can!
Step by spark-flung, leaping step,
Ranting wildly, orange flames
Dance in the rooftops, roar in the rooftops!
Snapping all the timbers, cracking all the walls!
London's towering walls of flame
Reach for the sky to set it burning.
Only the river flows on as before,
Quenching the ashes that rain on its shore.

The Great Fire of London was in September 1661.

The Box of Tricks

Into the box pack peace, and light:
A glowing calm
To hold back the darkness
And the unknown terrors of night.
Into the box pack warmth,
A crackling sizzle of cosy toasting
To warm the winter night.
The same box can hold
The pop of the homely stove
As the gas lights below the hopeful kettle.
The same box holds,
Holds by the dozen,
The troublesome cough,
Nagging, middle-aged cough
For the pointless, youthful folly
Which had money to burn.
Into the box pack wonder:
The wonder of a sky, lit with streaking fire,
Lights and sound in a bonfire glow:
The Bang! of a sudden thunderflash,
Shattered nerves of cats and dogs,
And sudden calls upon the fire brigade.
Into the box pack terror!
Terror across the meadows on a dry summer day
The galloping flames encircling, driven by the wind
Threatening the woods,
Fighting the beaters with eye-biting smoke.
Into the box pack horror!
The full horror of shattering glass
Of black smoke pouring into the sky,
The roaring of the house,
And the desolation of everything gone.
We could sell the box
For a few pence.

TREASON AND PLOT

Crowning the wood-ribbed cardboard mountain,
Lofty and lonely sits the guy:
King of the castle, guarded round, while
First stars peep from the darkening sky.

In gathering quiet and deepening darkness,
Whispering courtiers, hushed people wait.
Then cowardly, creepingly, pierce-bright flickerings
Move in the mountain with night-stabbing hate!

Solemnly still sits the king of the castle.
Running flames muster their snarling attack -
Jackal dogs! leaping in flaring and frenzy,
Drawing their courage and strength from the pack!

Silent he sits in the heat of the battle,
Heedless of smoke, and the wild, leaping light -
Powerless king, in the glare and the frenzy
Of frantic assassins, who crowd him from sight.

....

This is the low white pile of ash
Where the dogs of flame once stormed in power:
And the castled king of the cardboard mountain
Lies in the charcoal dust of his tower.

Night Light

The steady flame in the quiet night
Burns brightly, casting peaceful light
About the room; its trusted glow
Keeps watch upon the child below
Who lies asleep; the burning eye
Rebukes the draughts that sidle by
With a fluttered, silent shake of head,
As shadows shudder on the bed.
Then all is still. The candle flame,
Shining, counts all hours the same,
And constant in its proper place
Consumes the night at even pace.

Facts!

There was a young fellow from Kew
Who wrote all the facts that he knew
In less than a page.
In a frustrated rage
He cheated, and made up a few.

The Talk

We sat on the hard, wooden floor.
The talk was a bit of a bore.
We sat there all dumb
While our bottoms went numb,
And we tried very hard not to snore.

Lost Property

Mary had a little lamb
Its fleece was yellow-grey.
She took it with her round the school
But lost it on the way.
They found it by the changing rooms.
Alas, she hadn't named it.
They put it in 'lost property'
But Mary never claimed it.

Windbite

My feet are frozen, lost to feeling.
Frost it took my toes!
My nose is numb where the wind has gnawed it,
Rawly red it glows!
The edge on the air brings a tear to eye
As it cuts like steel from a leaden sky.
The dry leaves drift and frisk and fly
As the biting wind it blows.

Midwinter

The cold, grey sky
Sighs with a keen damp breath
Which the bare black twigs ignore.
And the hard, black arms stretch out,
Fingers pointing everywhere -
There! here! there!
Look at the ground, look at the sky!
See? It isn't! It's gone!
And the wet leaves lie lifeless
Trodden in the ground;
While the hidden sun,
Still travelling incognito
Slips finally away
In a dull, orange mist.

Slides

A cutting wind bit at my face
With sharp, cold, invisible teeth
Bringing water to my eyes. The winter air
Coated the walls, the fence tops, gates,
And the blades of grass with sugar-frosted whiteness:
While ears and fingers fast fell prey
To a sparkling air unbreakfasted.
The bicycles and cars felt their way
Warily on familiar roads
That would maim and murder that morning!
Cars and bikes don't like to play at slides.
Nice in the playground
But ice on the road
Can kill you coming to school!

REVIVALS

Sounds once uttered, songs once sung
Snared in motion by the magic wires,
Frozen in an instant, warm and vibrant:
Pressed and packed in plastic discs.
Voices, singers, twangy guitars,
Orchestras stored and preserved forever;
Scratchy voices from the distant past,
Swinging saxophones, sweet clarinets,
Banjos strumming in a long-dead Dixie;
Velvet voices once I loved,
Packaged, pressed, preserved in plastic.
Open them fresh as the day when made:
Remake the music long-since played.
John Brown's banjo may be busted into bits
But its sound stands ready to march!

Blizzard

Through a white, swirling, blinding mist,
We force our blinded windswept way.
The air is full of flying snow.
We cannot see the way we go.
But face to the storm,
Face to the wind,
Face to the stinging, whirling flakes
Two snowmen plod
Home to the warm:
Home to the warm, bright
Crackling fireside:
Home to tea, and toast and cakes.

A Day on the Ice

The ducks, disconsolate and dispossessed
Stood, mournful at the broken end of lake
Behind the island. All the rest was ice,
All smooth, and hard as glass, and ours to take!
Ours to dare! and test the water's skin!
We slipped and slid, and slung away our fears!
The wintry wind had given us the waters
Whose needle breath still pricked our eyes to tears.
The sparkle in the light was all for gladness!
We laughed and slithered, shouted, wild at play!
Our joyful shouts brought others there to join us:
A hundred larked upon the lake that day!
The skaters swirled, and scattered ice like sugar,
The growling skates cut into ringing ice.
The dark glass depth was clouded over crystals.
The surface creaked and shifted. Not so nice!

    A crack rang out. a tearing sound!
    'Quick, boys, quick! to firmer ground!'
    We fled. The water licked our feet.
    'The ice is breaking up! Retreat!'
All panicking we gained the shore
The lake was for the ducks once more.

The Frog-Prince

The handsome prince sat beside the pool
And cried salt tears for his lady fair:
For his dearest love and his heart's desire
Was a sweet young frog in the pool down there.
'Ah, woe is me for a wicked spell
And this human form that I'm forced to wear
When I would be glad and green again,
And a handsome frog for my lady fair!'

****

Now the King and queen thought the youth their son
(Who was truly lost in a long-since fog),
And they wondered why he should sit and moan
And long for the life of a carefree frog.
So they planned his match with a royal bride:
But he dived in the bath and he tried to hide.

****

The church was bright and the flowers were gay,
But the prince disappeared on his wedding day.
And they searched out wide in each park and wood,
And they dragged all the lakes, but it was no good.
Now some say he drowned when he tripped in a bog -
But the truth is, he slipped off to be a frog.

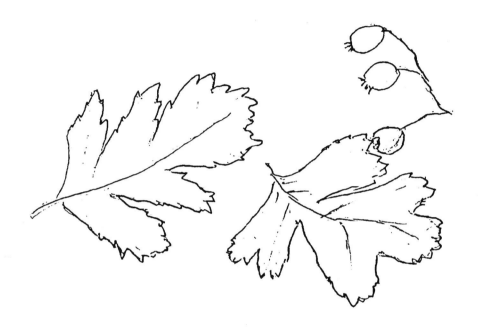

THORN HEDGE IN WINTER

Closed are the buds on the woody bare branches,
Sealed in their tightness, and proof against rain;
Trickling ditches: in barren, grey hedgerows
Which prickle and wait for the growing again.

Swept by the winds of the autumn and winter,
The spent leaves lie mouldering moistly below,
Where the bristling stocks of the hedgerow are gathered
To anchor the hillside in all winds that blow.

Sun Legend

All the winter the Sun had been hiding.
He had lain long abed, and got up late.
He had skulked around the skirts of the sky,
Avoiding looking straight at the Earth.
When he was glimpsed wandering in mists
He was weak and sickly, not himself.
Until one day as he looked down
He saw among the dead flowers of last year
The bright and sweet faces of primroses
Smiling hopefully up and around:
Brightening the gardens, cheering up the ground.
The Sun found himself, without knowing it, smiling.
Then he thought, 'You know, I feel better!'
And he began to beam again.

The sun is beaming in the blue

Spring is springing

How about you?

INDEX

Accident in the Sky	27	The Puddle Pounce	25
Autumn Leaves	52	Rabbits	45
Autumn Scrunch	53	Revivals	64
Battling the Air	9	Riverside Blues	40
Bedford Park Lake	15	The Rubble-Bubble Bounce	40
Before the Dawn	13	Sausages	42
Beginning in the End	5	Shoot!	51
Blizzard	65	Slide into Night	18
The Box of Tricks	57	Slides	63
The Bulldozers	17	Solomon Strong	41
The Cat	44	Sparrows at Dawn	11
The Classroom Ghost	55	Starlight	50
The Concrete Mixer	22	Stepping Stones	26
Daffodils	14	The Store wind	26
A Day on the Ice	66	The Swallow	37
The Dream of the Sea	33	Swan on the Falls	36
Dusk	46	Suburban Caterpillar	30
The Elm Tree's Doom	49	Sun Legend	69
Facts!	61	Surly Riser	38
Fishing	24	The Talk	61
The Frog Prince	67	Terry the Terrible	38
Garden Birds	29	Thorn Hedge in Winter	68
The Global View	35	Thundercloud	27
Gooseberry Jam	38	Tig	54
The Gusty Wind	6	Treason and Plot	59
High Summer	39	Treebop	47
House Mouse	43	Treesin the Wind	7
Journey of a Puddle	23	Tremors	19
Kite	9	The Troglodytes	24
London Fire	56	The Waking of the World	10
Lost Property	61	The Watercycle	31
Midwinter	62	Wellies	16
The Minnow	36	Wet Days	25
Mistle Thrush	11	Wet Homecoming	28
Mr. Hedgehog on the Beach	42	Wind and Rain	8
My Balloon	21	Windbite	62
Nightlight	60	Wind in the Town	7
The Primula	10	The Woollywoofer	44